To everyone who works collectively for human rights
—M.M.

With all my love to Paola, my home, my sky
—A.M.

Many, many thanks to Christy Regenhardt, former editor at the Eleanor Papers
Project of George Washington University, and Kirsten Strigel Carter,
Deputy Director and Supervisory Archivist of the FDR Presidential Library
and Museum, for their time and expertise.

Balzer + Bray is an imprint of HarperCollins Publishers.

Unshakable Eleanor: How Our 32nd First Lady Used Her Voice to Fight for Human Rights
Text copyright © 2024 by Michelle Markel
Illustrations copyright © 2024 by Alejandro Mesa
All rights reserved. Manufactured in Italy.
Library of Congress Control Number: 2023944144
ISBN 978-0-06-239847-5

Typography by Dana Fritts
24 25 26 27 28 RTLO 10 9 8 7 6 5 4 3 2 1
First Edition

UNSHAKABLE
Eleanor

How Our 32nd First Lady
Used Her Voice to Fight
for Human Rights

By Michelle Markel

Illustrated by Alejandro Mesa

Balzer + Bray
An Imprint of HarperCollinsPublishers

In fashionable New York,
where ladies go out in fine French dresses,
there lives a shy orphan named Eleanor.
Though her mother was a dazzling beauty,
Eleanor's not like her at all.
She's been told she's homely
and made to feel like a failure.

But Eleanor refuses to fail. Every night, she takes out her father's letters, full of love and hope. He wanted her to face her fears. He believed she'd grow into a brave, generous young woman. Over and over she reads his words, so she'll believe it too.

She takes those letters, like a good luck charm,
   to her finishing school across the sea,
where she excels at her studies,
helps other girls with theirs,
and even smacks her way onto the field hockey team.
Under her shyness, she finds a bolder Eleanor.

That's how, stomach in knots, she makes it through
  her debutante ball.
And how she volunteers to work with poor immigrants,
taking the streetcar and walking to the settlement house,
though most wealthy women wouldn't dare.
Eleanor teaches dance steps to a group of spirited girls
and loves it!
She's surprised by the things she can do.

As the wife of Franklin Delano Roosevelt, her distant cousin, she tries to be an ideal society lady. Hosting grand receptions, paying social calls, she helps her husband become a politician. But Eleanor knows she can do more!

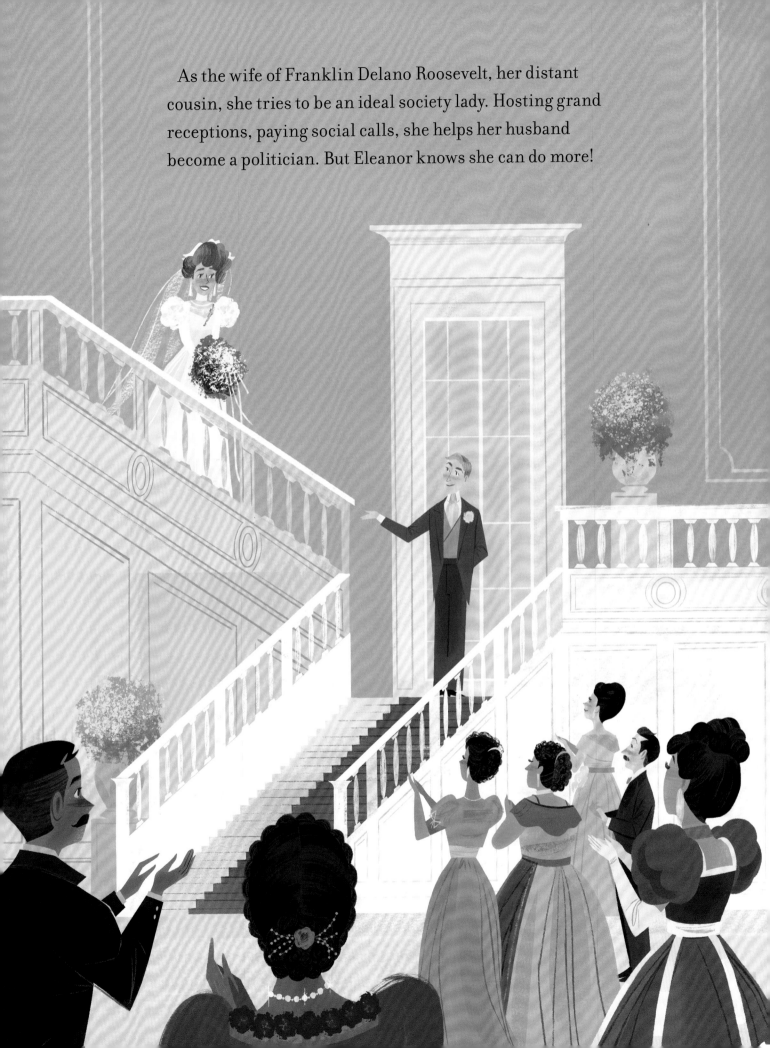

In the 1920s, she gets a chance. Many women are banding together to fight for social causes. Eleanor joins reformers trying to end child labor, unsafe conditions in factories, and other problems. And while Franklin recovers from polio, she works in politics to keep him in touch.

LABOR RIGHTS FOR ALL!

WOMEN SOLIDARITY

fair wages!

SAFE WORKING CONDITIONS

NEW YORK

Can she raise money? Yes.

Can she write newsletters? You bet.

Can she deliver a speech? At first, she loses her nerve. Her notes tremble in her hands. She wishes the ground would open up and swallow her.

But Eleanor learns to focus on the audience,
look into their eyes, and smile.
Soon she's winning over crowds!

Then Franklin reenters politics. And he's elected
president! Eleanor becomes First Lady—a hostess
at the White House! The whole country is watching.
She's terrified.

But as president, Franklin has a huge crisis to manage: the Great Depression. Millions of Americans are out of work. Many have to search garbage bins for food or stand in line for bread or soup. Franklin and his staff create job programs for men—who support most families. But Eleanor knows women need help too!

"I want you to write to me," she tells them in her new magazine column—and thousands do. She persuades Franklin to appoint women to high-ranking positions. Though she's nervous about it, Eleanor holds her own press conferences—just for women reporters.

And she travels from coast to coast, like no First Lady has done before.
Visiting impoverished areas and inspecting government projects called
the New Deal, Eleanor becomes a reporter for Franklin. She gives folks
a smile, asks them what they need.

One day Eleanor drives down to one of the poorest areas in the South,
a coal-mining camp in West Virginia,
where mothers wash and cook with filthy stream water,
and in the coal-dust-covered shacks on the hillside,
hungry children eat from bowls of scraps.

Eleanor is outraged—America's workers can't live
on starvation wages. With Franklin's approval,
she helps set up a homesteading project where the
miners can have decent homes and a better life.

But when it's time to pick the residents, Black people aren't allowed in. Officials exclude them, the community protests against them, other homesteaders vote them out.

Eleanor's the granddaughter of enslavers. Growing up, she heard stories about the Old South but not about white supremacy and the suffering it caused. Now she understands firsthand how much power racists have in America.

What can she do?

Across the nation, Black leaders are working for equality and justice, including Walter White of the NAACP and educator Mary McLeod Bethune.

Eleanor seeks their advice and becomes their friend.

She joins Walter's campaign for a law against the killing of Black people by white lynch mobs and promotes Mary for a top government post. Exchanging letters, having long talks, they let Eleanor know the struggles of Black Americans, how they're denied their full rights as citizens. It's been seventy years since the end of enslavement, but they're still treated as less than human.

Eleanor uses her position to help—in any way she can.

With Mary's encouragement,
she lets photographers take pictures of her
crossing the color line.

To many white citizens, especially in the South,
Eleanor's behavior is scandalous. She's always in the news,
rallying support for her causes. Some people think she's
overstepped her bounds, as a woman and as a First Lady.
Some say she's dangerous.

The press runs ugly cartoons,
the FBI tracks her activities,
the public sends vicious letters—
one even asks Franklin to chain Eleanor up and muzzle her.

But they can't crush her dreams. Bolder than ever, she exposes the mistreatment of poor workers—from maids to migrant fruit pickers. Always she looks for hope in programs like the National Youth Administration, where young men and women, regardless of race, learn job skills so they can find work one day.

The truth is, change is slow and painful.
Is she discouraged? Yes.
Will she give up?
Never.
Every small victory makes a difference.

When the United States enters World War II, and Japanese citizens are victims of racist attacks, Eleanor defends them as loyal Americans.

When Black soldiers in army camps
are given fewer privileges
than German prisoners of war,
she says,
"We can't defend democracy overseas
if we don't have it at home."

She visits Black pilots who demand to serve in combat,
showing the country she supports them,

and she cheers on women working in defense plants,
then helps them get childcare for their babies.

After Franklin dies, Eleanor is asked to serve her country at the newly created United Nations. She's not an experienced diplomat or scholar like the other delegates. To be honest, she's scared.

But she is chosen to lead a committee on the rights and freedoms of all human beings. They create a beautiful document to guide all governments on earth.

When it's approved, the general assembly rises and applauds Eleanor Roosevelt!
Who used to be shy. Who once trembled giving speeches.
Who's learned to stare down her fears.

THE UNIVERSAL DECLARATION OF **Human Rights**

Long job finished, Eleanor writes in her diary.
But she knows there's more work to be done—
to end injustice and inequality,
to spread love and respect.

"The future belongs to those who believe in the
beauty of their dreams . . . ,"
Eleanor says.
"But we cannot wait till tomorrow.
Tomorrow is now."

Timeline of Eleanor Roosevelt's Life and Her Work for Human Rights

1884—Anna Eleanor Roosevelt is born on October 11 in New York City, to Anna and Elliott Roosevelt.

1892—After her mother dies, Eleanor is cared for by her grandmother Mary Hall.

1894—Eleanor's father dies.

1899–1902—Attends Allenswood Academy in England.

1903—Joins the Junior League and starts teaching exercise and dancing at the Rivington Street Settlement House. Joins the National Consumers League and helps investigate working conditions in the garment industry.

1905—Marries Franklin Roosevelt on March 17.

1906—Has a daughter, Anna, on May 3.

1907—Her son James is born on December 23.

1909—Son Franklin Jr. is born on March 18 and dies the same year.

1910—Son Elliot is born on September 23. Franklin is elected to the New York State Senate.

1913—Franklin is appointed Assistant Secretary of the Navy. The Roosevelts move to Washington, DC.

1914—Eleanor's son Franklin Jr. is born on August 17.

1916—Her son John is born on March 17.

1917—The US enters World War I.

1918—Volunteers at naval hospitals and for the American Red Cross.

1919—Lobbies the interior secretary to improve conditions at St. Elizabeth's Hospital. Visits shell-shocked veterans.

1920—The Nineteenth Amendment gives women the right to suffrage, but literacy tests, poll taxes, and other requirements continue to suppress the votes of Black, Asian, and (in some states) Indigenous women. Joins the League of Women Voters. Begins public speaking.

1921—Nurses Franklin when he's stricken with polio. She publishes her first article for a national audience.

1922—Joins the Women's Trade Union League and works with the Women's Division of the New York State Democratic Committee.

1924—Organizes Democratic women across New York State. Chairs the women's platform of the Democratic National Committee. The Bureau of Investigation (now the FBI) begins to keep a file on her.

1925—Edits *Women's Democratic News*. She testifies before the New York State legislature on shorter hours for women and child workers.

1926—Co-purchases the Todhunter School and starts teaching history, literature, and current events there. Pickets with the the women paper-box makers and is charged with disorderly conduct.

1928—After Franklin is elected governor of New York, the Roosevelts move to Albany. Eleanor resigns from her political jobs.

1929—Inspects state institutions for Franklin. The stock market crashes, contributing to the Great Depression.

1932—Franklin is elected president.

1933—Initiates a weekly press conference for women reporters. Travels 40,000 miles as FDR's "ambassador," observing social and economic conditions. Begins advocating for the Arthurdale resettlement community in West Virginia. Chairs the White House conference on the Emergency Needs of Women. Starts writing a monthly column for *Women's Home Companion*.

1934—Begins advocating for Black Americans, passing their concerns to Franklin's administration. Joins the Washington, DC, chapters of the National Urban League and the NAACP. Addresses the National Conference on Negro Education.* Lobbies for anti-lynching legislation and old-age pensions.

---

* *Note*: In the past, Black Americans used the terms "colored" and "Negro" to self-identify. Today, these terms are considered unacceptable because of their association with enslavement and racism.

1934 (continued)—Hosts the White House Conference on Camps for Unemployed Women.

1935—Begins "My Day" newspaper column. Visits Howard University's Freedmen's Hospital and lobbies Congress for increased funding. Advocates for Mary McLeod Bethune's appointment as an adviser to the National Youth Administration.

1936—Supports the Southern Tenant Farmers Union. Franklin is reelected president.

1938—Helps organize the Southern Conference on Human Welfare in Birmingham, Alabama. At the conference, she challenges segregation laws by sitting in the aisle separating white and Black participants. Along with Mary McLeod Bethune, she convenes the White House Conference on Participation of Negro Women and Children in Federal Welfare Programs. She campaigns against the poll tax.

1939—When the Daughters of the American Revolution refuse to let Marian Anderson, a world-famous Black singer, perform in Constitution Hall, Eleanor resigns in protest. Walter White suggests the Lincoln Memorial as an alternate venue.

1940—Franklin is reelected president. Eleanor testifies before Congress in support of aid to migrant farmworkers. Urges Franklin to set up the Fair Employment Practices Commission.

1941–1945—US enters World War II. As racist public sentiment builds against Japanese Americans, Eleanor speaks out on their behalf. She tries in vain to stop Franklin from ordering thousands of Japanese Americans to move to internment camps. After they are evacuated, she advocates for them, passing their concerns about mistreatment in the camps to the War Relocation Authority, intervening for early releases, and helping individuals where she can. At the Tuskegee Army Air Field, Eleanor takes a flight with C. Alfred Anderson, instructor of the Black pilot training program. The 99th Pursuit Squadron is eager to serve, but like most Black servicemen, they are not sent on combat missions. Eleanor builds critical support for the airmen, who are deployed by Franklin in 1943 and go on to become highly decorated veterans.

1941–1945 (continued)—When Black labor leader A. Philip Randolph threatens a march on Washington to protest defense industry hiring practices, Eleanor takes his demands to Franklin. He issues an executive order banning discrimination on the basis of race, creed, color, or national origin.

1942—Advocates for women's employment in war industries.

1943—Visits 400,000 soldiers in the South Pacific. Helps create the first government-sponsored day care center. Helps integrate Sojourner Truth Housing Project in Detroit, and she is blamed for the riot it causes.

1944—Franklin is reelected.

1945—Pressures the Army Nurse Corps to admit Black women. Franklin dies on April 12. President Truman appoints Eleanor to UN delegation.

1947—Chairs the UN Human Rights Commission.

1948—Presents the Universal Declaration of Human Rights to the General Assembly for adoption.

1950s—Speaks to the UN on the political rights of women. In 1953, begins working for the American Association for the UN as a volunteer organizer, publicist, speaker, and fundraiser.

1955—Supports the Montgomery Bus Boycott and desegregation; she appears at a Madison Square Garden fundraiser with Martin Luther King Jr.

1957—The Ku Klux Klan places a $25,000 bounty on Eleanor's head.

1958—Drives through Klan country to deliver a workshop on civil disobedience at Highlander Folk School.

1959—Testifies before Congress in support of the minimum wage.

1961—Chairs the President's Commission on the Status of Women.

1962—Supports the Freedom Riders and chairs a commission of inquiry into attacks on civil rights workers. Dies from complications of tuberculosis on November 7.

Select Bibliography

Beasley, Maurine H., Holly C. Shulman, and Henry R. Beasley, eds. *The Eleanor Roosevelt Encyclopedia.*
   Westport, Conn.: Greenwood Press, 2001

Black, Allida M. *Casting Her Own Shadow: Eleanor Roosevelt and the Shaping of Postwar Liberalism.*
   New York: Columbia University Press, 1996.

——, ed. *What I Hope to Leave Behind: The Essential Essays of Eleanor Roosevelt.* Brooklyn, N.Y.: Carlson Pub., 1995.

Hoff-Wilson, Joan, and Marjorie Lightman, eds. *Without Precedent: The Life and Career of Eleanor Roosevelt.*
   Bloomington: Indiana University Press, 1984.

Kearns Goodwin, Doris. *No Ordinary Time: Franklin and Eleanor Roosevelt: The Home Front in World War II.*
   New York: Simon and Schuster, 1994.

Lash, Joseph P. *Eleanor and Franklin: The Story of Their Relationship, Based on Eleanor Roosevelt's Private Papers.*
   New York: W. W. Norton & Co., 1971.

Roosevelt, Eleanor. *The Autobiography of Eleanor Roosevelt.* New York: Harper Perennial Modern
   Classics; Reprint Edition: 2014.

——. *You Learn By Living.* New York: First Harper Perennial Olive Edition, 2016.

Ware, Susan. "Women and the Great Depression." *History Now* 17 (Spring 2009).
   https://bpb-us-e1.wpmucdn.com/blogs.uoregon.edu/dist/7/11428/files/2017/03/
        Ware-Women-and-the-Great-Depression-wtw4tk.pdf

Weiss, Nancy J. *Farewell to the Party of Lincoln: Black Politics in the Age of FDR.*
   Princeton, N.J.: Princeton University Press, 1983.

Wiesen Cook, Blanche. *Eleanor Roosevelt: Volume 1 1884–1933.* New York: Penguin, 1993.

——. *Eleanor Roosevelt: Volume 2, The Defining Years, 1933–1938.* New York: Viking, 1999.

——. *Eleanor Roosevelt: Volume 3: The War Years and After, 1939–1962.* New York: Viking, 2016.

Websites

Franklin D. Roosevelt Presidential Library and Museum: fdrlibrary.org/digitized-collections

The Eleanor Roosevelt Papers Project at George Washington University: erpapers.columbian.gwu.edu

More about People of Color and Women During the Depression

In the early twentieth century, racial discrimination was widespread. Most Black, Indigenous, and people of color had limited job opportunities and were hired for low-paying, low-status work. When the Depression hit, they were the first to be fired, and they sank even lower into poverty. In 1933, over 25 percent of the country was unemployed. But the jobless rate for people of color was 50 percent. For Black Americans in some areas, it was nearly 70 percent.

Racism made it harder for people of color to earn a living. Many white people believed that they should have priority for any available work. In some northern cities, they asked companies to fire Black Americans and replace them with white workers. In the west, migrant white workers took farm jobs that had belonged to Mexican Americans—many of them citizens—who then were rounded up and deported.

Because of gender bias, women workers also struggled during the Depression. Most Americans believed that jobs should go to men—the traditional breadwinners—while women took care of the household. At the start of 1933, an estimated two million women were unemployed, including some who supported their families. White women who lost their jobs in teaching, nursing, offices, and factories often became domestic workers, taking the jobs of women of color who had been unjustly fired.

People of Color and Women During the New Deal

President Roosevelt's administration did much to alleviate the crushing poverty of people of color—more than any other had before. It also provided work and relief to women. However, his recovery program, called the New Deal, did not address—and often reinforced—institutional racism in America, including Jim Crow laws in the South.

In the beginning, many people of color were excluded from New Deal programs because of their race, the types of jobs they held, or in some cases because they weren't US citizens. Those who did qualify often suffered discrimination. The majority of Black people lived in the South, where racist local administrators refused to provide jobs and aid or paid them less than whites and segregated them at work projects. After civil rights leaders criticized these and other inequities, some improvements were made.

Women found work in New Deal programs—though they had far fewer opportunities and typically received less pay than men. An unprecedented number were hired in leadership positions in government.

Despite its shortcomings, the New Deal provided hundreds of thousands of women and people of color with jobs and relief by the time the Depression ended.

Mary McLeod Bethune, Walter White, and the Roosevelt Administration

Mary McLeod Bethune (1875–1955) was an educator and civil rights advocate before serving as a New Deal official. In 1904, with a shoestring budget, she established the Daytona Literary and Industrial School for Training Negro Girls, which later became Bethune-Cookman College. She served as president of the National Association of Colored Women in 1924, and in 1935 she founded the National Council of Negro Women.

Bethune was arguably the most influential Black American adviser in President Roosevelt's administration. She made frequent visits to the White House, where she provided the president, and especially Eleanor, with suggestions on how to address the plight of African Americans. She became the first African American in charge of a federal agency: the Negro division of the National Youth Administration, which focused on two of her greatest concerns—work and education for young people. Bethune was also the leader of the president's Black Cabinet, which informally counseled him on race-related matters. Her influence and access to the Roosevelt administration gave hope to the African American community.

Walter White (1893–1955) was a civil rights activist, investigator, and writer. In 1918 he began working for the National Association for the Advancement of Colored People (NAACP). Because of his light skin, he was able to pass as a white reporter to investigate lynchings and race riots, which he later publicized in his writings. In 1931, he became executive secretary of the NAACP, a job he held until his death in 1955.

White waged a long campaign for the passage of anti-lynching legislation. Eleanor arranged for him to meet the president—who was not persuaded to endorse the cause, for fear of alienating powerful Southern Democrats. Afterward, White often corresponded with the First Lady, educating her about matters of race and enlisting her support. Representing the NAACP, he argued for greater participation of Black Americans in New Deal programs. During World War II, White and labor leader A. Philip Randolph persuaded FDR to issue an order banning discrimination in defense programs and to establish the Fair Employment Practices Committee.